The Quacky Duck Heist

Marcy Schaaf

To my brother Joe,

The funniest kid ever and to all best friends everywhere.

The bond between best friends is a treasure, filled with laughter, adventures, and unforgettable memories.

This book is for those who know the joy and mischief that comes from having a true best friend by their side.

May you always cherish the special moments and find joy in the simple things, just like Joe and Franky did.

With all my love.
Your little sister
Marcy Schaaf

Best friends Joe and Franky
lived in Flint, Michigan.

They loved riding their bikes to the pond.

One sunny day, Joe had a funny idea.

“Let's catch some ducks for our pond!”
he said

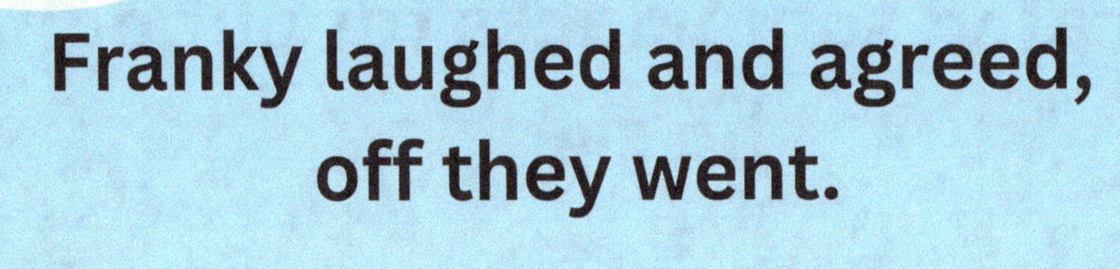

Franky laughed and agreed,
off they went.

They jumped into the water,
splashing about.

Joe began to pulled ducks under by their feet.

They carefully stuffed the
ducks into bags.

With ducks in tow
they rode back home.

Joe and Franky had a pond
in the back yard.

"We'll have pet ducks,"
Joe said, excitedly.

But the ducks had different plans.

In the morning, the ducks flew away.

Joe and Franky were
puzzled and frustrated.

"Why don't they stay?"
Joe wondered aloud.

Franky shrugged, scratching his head thoughtfully.

“We should ask Grandpa,”
Franky suggested.

Grandpa laughed,
hearing their duck tale.

“Ducks need to feel safe to stay.”

"And ducks need a life partner too."

“You’ll need one girl and one boy duck.”

"To tell them apart look at their feathers."

"Boy ducks have bright colors
girls are plain."

Joe and Franky understood the lesson.

They decided to make the pond nicer.

With plants and rocks, it looked lovely.

Some ducks started staying, feeling safe.

People need to feel safe to stay in our lives too, just like ducks!

The End!

Books By Schaaf

www.BookBySchaaf.com

Find us at:

www.ingramcontent.com/pod-product-compliance
Lightning Source LLC
Chambersburg PA
CBHW082106130726
48003CB00009BA/3071